R00311 69918

CHICAGO PUBLIC LIBRARY
HAROLD WASHINGTON LIBRARY CENTER

R0031169918

REF
LB
2331.4
.G68   Government and
          academia

DATE		
REFERENCE		

FORM 125 M

Cop. 1   SOCIAL SCIENCES AND HISTORY DIVISION

The Chicago Public Library

Received   MAR 30 1980

FORM 125 M

GOVERNMENT AND ACADEMIA: THE UNEASY BOND

John Charles Daly, *Moderator*

Robert A. Goldwin
Stephen Graubard
David Mathews
Robert Wood

A Round Table held on April 13, 1978
and sponsored by
the American Enterprise Institute
for Public Policy Research
Washington, D.C.

This pamphlet contains the edited transcript of
one of a series of AEI forums.
These forums offer a medium for
informal exchanges of ideas on current policy problems
of national and international import.
As part of AEI's program of providing opportunities
for the presentation of competing views,
they serve to enhance the prospect
that decisions within our democracy will be based
on a more informed public opinion.
AEI forums are also available on
audio and color-video cassettes.

AEI Forum 19

© 1978 by American Enterprise Institute
for Public Policy Research, Washington, D.C.
Permission to quote from
or reproduce materials in this publication is granted
when due acknowledgment is made.
Views expressed in the publications of
the American Enterprise Institute are those
of the authors and do not necessarily reflect
the views of the staff, advisory panels,
officers, or trustees of AEI.

ISBN 0-8447-2136-0
Library of Congress Catalog Card No.78–19810

Printed in United States of America

JOHN CHARLES DALY, former ABC News executive and forum moderator: This Public Policy Forum, part of a series presented by the American Enterprise Institute, is concerned with Government and Academia: The Uneasy Bond.

Twenty years ago, when Congress debated the National Defense Education Act, Senator Barry Goldwater noted what in modern argot might be called the "camel's nose in the tent" syndrome. He prophesied that, if adopted, the legislation would mark the beginning of financial support, supervision, and ultimately control of education by federal authorities.

On the basis of the experience of these past twenty years or so, there is growing fear in academia that Senator Goldwater may have been right.

Although there are at least a dozen major pieces of federal legislation now governing various aspects of college and university life, there is no historic act of Congress mandating federal scrutiny of higher education; there is no government agency that has as its mission the regulation and supervision of the academy. Indeed, a substantial area of friction between the academy and government concerns the academy's accountability for public funds and its compliance with laws and regulations, such as the Occupational Safety and Health Act and minimum wage laws to which all corporate entities and employers are subject.

The basic uneasiness of the academy, however, results from its perception of the government as a menace to aca-

1

demic freedom. The education establishment is concerned about government intrusion into such areas as faculty hiring, student admissions, curriculum, and research, which Harvard's Derek Bok calls "the principal academic functions of higher education."

The primary menace in the conflict may well be affirmative action—a labyrinth of laws, directives, and regulations that circumscribe and sometimes compromise historic rights of the academy. Many in the educational community think universities and colleges today are used as instruments for the pursuit of social gains that have little or no relationship to quality education.

Dr. Mathews, as a former secretary of HEW and president of the University of Alabama, you have confronted the uneasy bond between academia and government from both perspectives. In your opinion just how burdensome is regulation, federal and state, on the academy?

DAVID MATHEWS: Probably the best words to describe the effects of regulation would be "excessively burdensome," but this uneasy bond is nothing new. For an educational community to assert that it has all of a sudden been invaded by the public domain is to forget its history.

If the bond is uneasy, it has always been so. Educational institutions are not self-generating; they are creations of society chartered to serve certain purposes. They have always been very much entwined with the public will, and I think properly so. That, in fact, has given them much of their vitality.

I do not decry affirmative action or any efforts of government to direct education onto paths that are socially meaningful. But I do question the methods we are currently using. I question them, not only on the grounds of what they are doing to the academic community, but on the grounds of what they are doing to the government. And I have come to the conclusion that much of the intrusion is counterproductive, from the viewpoint of both the institutions involved and the public.

MR. DALY: Dr. Wood, you have served as secretary of HUD, and as president of the University of Massachusetts. In your opinion, do institutions of higher education warrant exemption from the kinds of regulation that are imposed on other institutions in our society?

ROBERT WOOD: No, they do not. They do, however, warrant understanding for the kind of special, strange creatures they are. There are many distinctive features of the academy that should be taken into account: its complexity, its public-private mix, its division into colleges and universities, and its history, which, in the case of land-grant universities, consists of a hundred years of cordial and symbiotic relations with the Department of Agriculture and other federal agencies.

But the academy cannot claim a special exemption from the society's, or from the government's, goals of equality, openness, and fairness.

MR. DALY: Dr. Goldwin, you are the former dean of St. John's College in Annapolis, Maryland, whose curriculum leadership is legendary. Do you feel the government has honored the stern provision in federal education statutes that bars any department, agency, officer, or employee of the United States from exercising direct supervision or control over higher education?

ROBERT GOLDWIN: No, it has not. As a matter of fact, it is an impossible pledge to honor. There is no way that the government can accomplish what it intends to accomplish through regulation without exercising some control and without interfering somewhat in the essential activities of a college or a university.

I agree with David Mathews that the relationship of government and educational institutions is a very old one, as old as society. But today that bond consists of a very strange and excessive mixture of government action with educational enterprise, which I think is dangerous.

MR. DALY: Dr. Graubard, as a professor and the distinguished editor of an educational journal, what do you think has been the effect of social regulations requiring equal treatment of the sexes, affirmative action, and controls on scientific experimentation?

STEPHEN GRAUBARD: They have had several effects, the most important of which has been to change the complexion of student bodies in universities in certain ways. I speak of complexion not only in racial terms, but in other terms as well. For instance, the complexion of faculties has changed, and students and faculties have become aware of the loss of desirable conditions that existed before government regulations.

Most importantly, as a result of regulation of experimentation and other such matters—and as you know, regulation is based upon hundreds of different legislative and administrative acts—people have become aware of the federal presence in higher education in a way that they had not been before. There was no such presence before. Public institutions were always aware of what state legislators and state bodies did, but in the year 1930 nobody thought much about what Herbert Hoover was doing with respect to universities. Perhaps nobody thought much about anything Hoover did in those days; in any case, it is obvious that such regulation as we know today simply did not exist before just a decade ago.

Mr. Daly: Charles Saunders, the director of governmental relations at the American Council on Education, says that the challenge facing American universities is not merely to learn how to cope with federal regulation, but to develop new mechanisms for self-regulation. Is there an answer in his statement to the problems which you gentlemen face? Apparently, you feel that even though some federal participation is warranted, the methodology and perhaps the frames of reference are getting to be intrusive.

Dr. Graubard: There is no question that, at an earlier time, colleges and universities had the opportunity to regulate themselves in order to achieve the kinds of aims the federal government and other public bodies are now imposing upon them.

For complex historical reasons that I shall not try to enumerate, only minor efforts were made in this regard. Inevitably, many of the now existing regulations were then imposed.

There is no question that many within universities and outside them are very dubious about certain of these regulations, but in some instances it is very hard to change them. In other instances, it is hard to get agreement on alternatives that would achieve the same objectives. And in some instances, there is simply a constant insistence that the regulations are not working, but no political protest is made to the legislators. In other words, some individuals and groups are unhappy, but they do not translate this unhappiness into political protest that would make legislators or administrators move in another direction.

Dr. Wood: It might help if we got a little more specific about what, from the academic viewpoint, seems to hurt and what seems acceptable.

I think it is clear that most of our faculties have been very grateful for federal research dollars over the years, beginning with agriculture after World War II, and later in the sciences and engineering.

Indeed, between a fifth and a quarter of the budgets of the large research universities comes from this source, and universities have reluctantly come to understand and deal with the so-called red tape involved in handling research grants and contracts. University presidents have even become inured to the fact that the priorities of the university go out the window when a distinguished faculty member obtains a $2 million grant from Washington on his own. That part is accepted reasonably well. Where the rub comes, of course, is the point Mr. Daly mentioned earlier. Affirmative action, in particular, flies in the face of what has always been regarded in faculty life as "peer-group prerogative." Of all the faculty members of the universities in this country, women made up 19 percent in 1960 and 19.1 percent in 1972. Both in the recruitment of women and in the recruitment of blacks, there has been a thoroughly conservative, stand-pat attitude on the part of universities and colleges in this country.

DR. GOLDWIN: Some analyses have been made of why that is so—why, with all of the affirmative action efforts, the numbers of women in academic positions have not increased. It is not for lack of legislation and efforts at promoting female participation.

DR. WOOD: Well, in the decade I just referred to, the number of women Ph.D. graduates doubled while the percentage of women faculty stayed constant.

It is quite true that if we had paid attention to affirmative action in the 1960s, when we were growing, it would have been much easier to implement than it is in the 1970s, when we are retrenching. And I am aware of the argument that we may be tampering with meritocracy if we decide to adopt affirmative action goals. But, by and large, I think our profession has had a miserable record in the areas of self-discipline and self-regulation.

DR. GOLDWIN: I had in mind Thomas Sowell's research on this subject. He studied single academic women and compared them with men of the same age with the same quality of degree and numbers of publications. He showed that the single women get promoted, get tenure, and are paid as well as, or even a little better than, comparable men.

The big difference is between academic men and *married* academic women. Sowell came to the conclusion that when a single academic woman gets married, she has less time for her career. When a single academic man gets married, he has more time for his career. Thus, his situation improves while hers deteriorates. What kind of legislation will change that?

DR. WOOD: I'm neither a woman nor a member of a minority and I hesitate to take on the case of feminism, but I do—

DR. GOLDWIN: Sowell didn't say that he liked that situation, but he thought it explained quite a bit.

DR. WOOD: —but I do think these are valid concerns. Let's move from women and minorities to the handicapped program, which, when I left the University, had just dumped a $5 million facilities bill on us. I think there are legitimate complaints about the bureaucratic nature of government intervention. Dr. Mathews and I are both familiar with the incapacity of federal agencies to say anything that is clear-cut or that can be followed. But that's a different battle. My basic point is that this country is unique in saying that the way people gain opportunities is through education. If we have made that our bedrock political value, and if, over the years, we have systematically denied opportunities to minorities and to women, then we have asked for the kind of regulation problem we've gotten into.

DR. MATHEWS: Yes, but I think the argument is past that point. I think the argument now is, given the desire to open the professional ranks to people who for one reason or another have been excluded, what kinds of approaches work?

The assumption we made in the 1960s—that we could solve the problem by simply passing a law and setting up a bureaucratic procedure—is under attack.

I don't think it fair to dismiss that attack by saying that the people who wish to question the effectiveness of the methods question the goals. We have to look seriously at the proposition that the way we are going about regulating higher education, even if we agree on the ends, is open to very serious question.

I cannot find any great evidence that the federal government's approach to the problem has always moved us forward. In fact, the statistics we have cited here are themselves an indictment of the federal processes.

MR. DALY: Would you catalog some of the areas where you feel the government is going about things the wrong way?

DR. MATHEWS: Well, for one thing, we have substituted a process for results. We do not judge results now, we judge the process. We say the results are too hard to judge, so we will judge the process instead.

By judging process and not results we have shifted the values and the focus, as well as the behavior of the bureaucracy.

Universities are now going through many new processes, which have not brought about any material change in the goals that we thought were important.

We have, in fact, substituted bureaucratic behavior for moral conviction, and I think that's to be regretted.

MR. DALY: Let's break this down into what I consider to be the major areas of housekeeping and hardware, and the very sensitive area of intrusion upon academic freedom.

Let's consider the hardware areas first. With so much government funding going to the universities and colleges, is it not inevitable that a government agency would be charged with making sure the money was spent for the purposes for which it was assigned and with evaluating whether or not it had produced fruitful results? Is there anything wrong with the basic premise that the government, as a prudent manager, has the right to do these things? If not, where has the government overdone it? Why are there complaints?

DR. GRAUBARD: There is no question that the government has the right, in this respect, to treat academic institutions as it would treat other institutions with which it has a contract.

The real question is a different one. Many businesses, for example, are able to stand government intrusion, and they can pass on to the consumer the additional costs of that intrusion in larger employee payrolls, in larger regulatory agencies that they appoint themselves for that purpose. In the case of academic institutions, the additional costs are also passed on, sometimes in higher tuition fees.

What is significant to me is that academic institutions increasingly regret and resent this intrusion, which adds expense and personnel that they would, in many instances, rather not have to pay for. It may, in some instances, even cause them to hire a person who is essentially an administrator, when in fact they would prefer to hire a teacher. All that is causing some to complain loudly.

The questions I would pose, however, are: Do we really know who is being hurt by this? and, How deep is the financial hurt? Is it not a fact that academic institutions are financially hurt by any number of other things that government does? For instance, they are hurt by the government's inability to control inflation, and by the problem of civil disorder in our cities and on campuses, which is infinitely more serious than anything that existed before, and which adds immeasurably to the expense of maintaining order on those campuses. Furthermore, I suspect that if we looked at the budgets of most colleges and universities, we would find that they are paying more for fuel—that their additional fuel bill is out of all proportion to the additional bill that they are paying for all the regulations they are exposed to.

The question, then, is a very simple one. It is not very pleasant to have to do some of these things, but how expensive is it really? And again, what is so interesting is that we do not have very much information in this area.

MR. DALY: We in Washington are continually interested in a debate that has been going on in Congress for some time, a thesis of which is that the costs of higher education have now reached the point where only the very poor and the very rich can afford it. And the elements that we have been discussing are all contributors to higher cost.

Dr. Mathews, you are the president of a university. Does the financial element so heavily weigh upon your abilities to add courses or improve courses that the university-college community warrants an exemption from, for instance, the handicapped regulations—

DR. MATHEWS: Before I answer, I would like to return to your original question and disagree with my colleague in order to support his argument.

MR. DALY: I like that. [Laughter.]

DR. MATHEWS: When we ask if the government has the right to look after the taxpayers, the educator will invariably say, "Of course." But in doing that, he swallows a proposition that he should not swallow, for the question is not just whether the government has the right, but whether it can carry out its responsibility effectively. The government, in carrying out its responsibility, has a responsibility not only to be right but also to be effective.

The science of government has not progressed to the point where the tools that are now available for accounting and surveillance have the precision of a scalpel! In fact, by injecting itself into the process, the government very often contaminates the academic environment and destroys those forces that are working to remedy problems.

And it is inappropriate to condemn the government on the grounds that universities are different from businesses and cannot pass on the costs. To frame the question that way is to miss the point—that the government is ineffective in what it does. I think Dr. Graubard has a very good argument, but I encourage him to frame it a little bit differently.

From both the institutional interest and the public interest, to separate the interest of the government from the interest of the public is to make a mistake.

DR. GOLDWIN: There is another problem with the efforts of Congress and the executive branch to find out whether they are getting their money's worth in the field of education.

Universities and colleges have many different objectives. Part of what they do is provide services to the public and to different government agencies. And in that context, they ought to be treated as any other contractor.

They also have a responsibility for handing down our heritage and culture, a process that used to be called "Americanization." But any good university or college also has another mission which is probably the most important of all, and that is an unqualified search for the truth. And when I say "unqualified," I mean not just in an American, or British, or Soviet context. There is no such thing as Soviet truth or British truth.

The real work of a college or university is a rather mysterious enterprise that is not suited to government control. And there is no way that any legislative body, even "the greatest deliberative body in the world," can find out if it is getting its money's worth. When it tries to, it distorts the whole enterprise.

MR. DALY: We are talking about effectiveness here, specifically the effectiveness of the government and its ultimate ability to make judgments. But the Inspector General of HEW reported that more than one-third of the $1.2 billion in research contracts in fiscal 1977 was inadequately accounted for by the universities and colleges. In fiscal 1976, according to the General Accounting Office estimate, the Veterans Administration disbursed $823 million in GI benefits to ineligible persons, chiefly because the recipients in the schools failed to fulfill their reporting responsibilities to VA on individual student status. So how effective is the university?

DR. WOOD: There are two things to be said here. First, Dr. Mathews is so eloquent at times that one hardly dares to examine his logic, but in this instance to categorize all of government as ineffective is probably going a little too far.

Second, the VA figures Mr. Daly cited represented an extremely dumb position of an extremely dumb agency. They really wanted us to take attendance in classes.

But, on the other side, remember that the academy is a pretty loose and strange organization itself. It persistently resists any administrative tidying. Professors believe that if they have a grant, no one should question their right to make long-distance calls or have a WATS line. They believe that their search for truth will be impaired if they keep any records at all.

That is essentially what universities are like after a period of rapid growth. Remember that in 1940, 11 percent of Americans went on to college; now 45 to 50 percent go. An enormous transformation has occurred.

We are a labor-intensive industry filled with workers who are essentially professional. Most of them are neurotic, creative, very untidy individuals, and more than half have tenure. And when considering how to deal with an equipment budget, remember that university research laboratories obsolesce at twice the rate of any industrial firm.

So we have complications, as well as elements of community. This outfit cannot be expected to be tidy. On the other hand, it can be expected to address some of the fundamental American rights, and that's a point where I feel most disappointed in our behavior.

DR. GRAUBARD: I think that if we really examine the compliance of many institutions, many of whom have had substantial experience with the federal government, we will find that they're not all as untidy as Dr. Wood suggests.

There are a number of institutions in this country at present that I would call federal grant universities. If a sufficient number of agencies in the federal government were, for whatever reason, suddenly to become disenchanted with them, they would literally have to close their doors in a way that many more modest colleges would not.

So, a fair number of them are very able to handle the regulatory system that exists. But that doesn't prevent some of them from feeling and expressing a great concern with the way the regulation is carried out.

And sometimes, particularly when it touches matters of appointment (since for any good university the heart of the system is the character of its faculty), there is bound to be a certain amount of noise.

But again, what surprises me is that, although there has been a certain amount of noise—and those of us who live in academic institutions are aware of it—so far it has not translated into political action. Apparently, there is not a vast public that feels the universities are, in fact, being significantly altered in unacceptable ways.

That is why I make a plea for much greater inquiry into this area. I think it is very important for us to understand what the social consequences of regulation are.

We need to know a great deal more about what is happening to private institutions as a result of the various kinds of regulations. We need to know what is happening to a lower-middle-class family's capacity to choose between private and public institutions, or to choose to send its children to any institution of higher learning.

We need to know a great deal more about how government appropriations are affecting certain of the major disciplines.

Unfortunately, we still lack the knowledge that makes it possible to answer even some of the most basic questions in all these areas. And that is one of the reasons why we find so many differences of opinion in this country. The factual base is very weak indeed.

DR. MATHEWS: I must commend Dr. Wood for his useful warning. But I still insist that the untidiness in the universities is no greater than the untidiness in the government's accounting methods. To say that the universities have failed to measure up to a certain standard of accounting conjures up in one's mind the kind of fixed standard that is set by the bar in the high jump.

There are different kinds of accounting standards, many of which are imprecise or arbitrary. The untidiness within the university is no worse than that within the government.

Another point needs to be made. We are discussing the involvement of the federal government as if it alone were doing something very peculiar by causing bureaucratization in the university. We are talking about bureaucratization as if it were imposed by the federal government or by the state government, but if we are honest, we will have to admit that bureaucratization is something that we have done to ourselves within institutions, and within systems of institutions, and within educational bureaucracies at every level.

Unless we correct and challenge this penchant to bureaucratize we will not deliver ourselves from what afflicts us. To attend to it at one point and not at another is to fail to understand what causes our dilemma.

Dr. Goldwin: Do you really favor the debureaucratization of the university?

Dr. Mathews: Indeed I do.

Dr. Goldwin: And what would you do about the University of Alabama? For instance, I would recommend that its size be reduced by nine-tenths, because no one has figured out a way to conduct the work of the university as an educational community, given the giant size of the institution.

It would not be fair to argue, as some people do, that no decent education takes place in these large institutions. What does happen is that talented human beings figure out how to make small communities within the big institutions. They figure out ways to evade the bureaucratic regulations, the red tape, and all the restrictions that come inevitably with size. But that can only be accomplished by small enclaves in the biggest institutions. I really don't know how we can reduce the level of bureaucratization without reducing size.

DR. WOOD: That's a classic dilemma of organizations in a large society. It is important to realize that an institution like the University of Massachusetts, for example, with three campuses, seven posts, camps, and stations, 32,000 students, 2,800 faculty members, and 4,982 other staff, is at least as complicated an institution as a multinational corporation.

We have headquarters in field, we have accountability in hierarchy because we use public money, and we are supposed to have community. We also now have labor relations and collective bargaining. That's a very complicated enterprise to make function. But the answer is not to break it up.

The same argument applies to medicine. Do we want first-rate tertiary hospitals, or do we want to go back to first-aid stations? We can make the same argument about laboratories.

We must somehow find ways to make that institution function, and I guess my argument is really that we have only come lately on the scene. We have usually tolerated management by amateurs in education. We made a man a dean because he didn't write his journal article on time, and then we made him a provost because he was unpopular with the department chairman.

There is a need for some professional management in the academic area, though it goes very much against our tradition. We still like to think about Mr. Chips; it seems the man is preeminent.

As a final note, I would say that all of what we've been talking about are real and serious problems, particularly federal government intrusion, but for most colleges and universities, both public and private, the critical relationship is with the state government.

As private institutions begin looking to state government, and as public institutions undertake to maintain their independence, continuing our pursuit of truth remains the university's basic mission.

And we are far more likely to have difficulty with the state houses and state legislatures than with the President and the Congress.

MR. DALY: Considering the limited time we have for this discussion, let's move away from the hardware and the accounting procedures and come to the sensitive area of academic freedom. What does the term "academic freedom" mean? Is it possible to arrive at a definition that can be used, for instance, by government to draw a line beyond which it could not pass? Who will define academic freedom?

DR. GOLDWIN: I would not try to define it, but I can talk about it.

There is no doubt that in any society the public has a tremendous interest in the quality of education and in the research that goes on. No society can claim to be outstanding or great if it does not have a great intellectual heritage that influences the whole society. The big question is, What can the government or any organization that is outside the academic sphere do to foster it?

One of the best things it can do is to keep its hands off. At least that has been the experience in the United States and in much of the Western world. When a government tries to encourage, direct, or steer the academic enterprise for the public good, it usually messes things up and often exercises a restraining effect, because one of the mysteries of the educational process is that we never know where the important findings are going to come from.

I understand academic freedom to mean the best that the community can do to help education, that is, by and large, leaving the universities pretty much to their own devices and not telling them what to study or what conclusions to come to.

MR. DALY: All right, let's come right to the point. Is the federal government invading the academic freedoms?

DR. GRAUBARD: I will try to answer that, and I will begin with a reminder that the tradition of academic freedom goes back a very long time, to the beginnings of the university. The university was once an independent corporation, a corporation into which the state could not intrude.

Gradually, through this freedom, an extraordinary scholarship developed, which, not always but at times, has been centered in universities.

We must remember today that for most of the history of universities the great donors to scholarship were not necessarily public bodies, particularly in this country; sometimes they were individuals.

But for the first time, given the expense of scholarship, it has turned out that in certain fields, particularly in some of the sciences, the federal government is the primary donor.

And one question has come up insistently from groups that do have access to their federal legislators and other political persons. For an activity that is essentially publicly funded, in which there is a clear public interest, and where there must be social consequences, is there some need to change the old form of contract between the researcher and the society, which was a contract not of absolute freedom, but of very considerable freedom?

For example, one of the dilemmas that has recently been discussed in the journal that I edit, *Daedalus*, is the following: let us imagine that a medical researcher could discover a way to prolong the lives of most of the people in this room by twenty or thirty years, but that those twenty or thirty years would be lived in what we would call a vegetable-like existence. We would be alive, but we would not be very active, and we certainly would not be working.

We would not be productive members of our society in any sense.

The author, Robert Morison, asks a very simple question in *Daedalus*: Is that a form of research that the society could attempt to stop? How would the society know how to stop it? Has it any right to stop it? Who would determine that?

I think a great many such questions are beginning to come into view—this is what the whole controversy on DNA is about.

DR. WOOD: The DNA controversy confronts the issue head on. Should we allow that kind of life-creating research to go on? If so, under what standards of control? Should it be under the control of the community, the university, the federal or state government? That issue will have to be faced within the next two or three years.

MR. DALY: Specifically, in terms of allowing the research or in terms of denying funds to continue the research?

DR. GRAUBARD: Of allowing the research. We will have to decide whether or not the social consequences are too hazardous. In other words, we must find out whether there really is a public interest, for there are public groups who insist that certain forms of research are too dangerous to undertake.

MR. DALY: And, therefore, this would be a reasonable area in which to consider whether academic freedom was being invaded.

DR. GRAUBARD: The scientific community itself would be split on this, with the overwhelming majority, I think, feeling that the original contract, which has worked for most of history, should be maintained.

That is what is so important—that the scientific community feels that way. But individual groups have asserted themselves in various cities where there are major laboratories intending to do such research.

MR. DALY: Will you explain DNA very briefly for the audience?

DR. GRAUBARD: This is new research which is thought to create the possibility of the generation of mutants that could be very dangerous. They could, in time, have infectious and other unknown consequences that pose dangers to life.

MR. DALY: All right. Let's return to the question. Where is academic freedom being invaded? There is the case of the government's attempt to force medical schools to admit third-year students who have studied abroad. Will somebody address that and tell me whether it was an unwarranted and possibly illegal intrusion by government?

DR. MATHEWS: We sound as if we are trying to decide whether our present condition is different from that in a Land of Oz. The Land of Oz never existed, and I really don't see the point of trying to decide whether we were ever in some place that never was.

The notion that the academy was once separate from the state is not supported by good evidence. The academy and the community have always been bound together.

DR. WOOD: Do you view the community as the state?

DR. GRAUBARD: The community in this case is the state. Do you know of the history of medieval Cambridge and medieval Oxford?

Dr. Mathews: I have studied it with some care.

Dr. Graubard: And do you know what the powers of the king were with respect to medieval Oxford and Cambridge?

Dr. Mathews: There was a contest between two centers of power: one the church, and the other the monarchy.

Dr. Graubard: Which period are you speaking of, Dr. Mathews?

Dr. Mathews: The twelfth and most particularly the thirteenth century—

Dr. Graubard: In the twelfth and thirteenth centuries, what was the king's power with respect to the University of Cambridge or Oxford?

Dr. Mathews: The kings tended to try to substitute their patronage for patronage (and power) already exercised by the church.

Dr. Graubard: The church was a state power, sir?

Dr. Mathews: Of course it was.

Dr. Graubard: Well, I must say that that will surprise many of our listeners.

Dr. Mathews: The only surprises should be in the broad interpretation I am giving to the term "state." The point I want to make is that the academy has always been bonded to society. At times higher education has been supported by the church, at times by the king, and at times by the National Institutes of Health, but despite the differences in "theology" between those three parties, they are in fact organizations that society has used to influence the academic community in various ways.

For us to take the position that we are guarding our purity makes it impossible for us to create the kind of political alliance that my basically correct colleague wishes to establish.

The best way to talk about our freedom is to say that we need only the kind of latitude to do the things that we were chartered to do for society. Raw and undigested political forces, whether they be of church or state or NIH, must not so interfere with what we do not just because of our interests but because of society's.

To talk that way is to understand our history. More to the point, it allows others who have similar concerns about overregulation to join with us in getting some relief. If we persist in viewing ourselves as separate and distinct, we make it impossible politically to form alliances that will give some relief to the academy.

DR. GRAUBARD: Dr. Mathews, nobody said that we were talking about something separate and distinct, that had no relation to the community.

Rather, I am talking about something that you, as a head of a state institution, know to have been true. For the whole of the nineteenth century, these state universities were concerned with a certain kind of independence from the state legislature. There were various devices for securing that independence. Boards of trustees were used for this purpose, and when they were too much under the influence of state authority, it was felt that in some way the authority of the university was being vitiated.

For a very long time scientists and most other scholars could pursue their research unhindered, which was, as was said here earlier, an inquiry into the truth. They were permitted to pursue that inquiry unhindered. At times there were various kinds of intervention, and those interventions were often followed by complaints from those who believed that the university had a different tradition.

It simply cannot be argued that the university has been under the control of others, mixing up church and state, to make it appear that the church is the state. Even in the seventeenth and eighteenth centuries in this country, the university was not free of the community. Nobody has suggested that. Nobody has insisted upon the university's right to be an ivory tower. That offensive term which is commonly used to describe the university is simply not accurate.

But there is a difference between being an ivory tower and being essentially the agency of the state. And in the nineteenth century, for example, when various university systems were contrasted, they were often contrasted precisely on that basis.

The University of Moscow created in 1755 was different from the University of Oxford or Cambridge in the eighteenth, nineteenth, and twentieth centuries.

DR. GOLDWIN: I agree with Dr. Mathews on one very important point, that any educational institution is not only bonded to the society, but also a creature of the society. It has no independent means of support. It gets its substance either from the government or from elements of the society, but it has no way of sustaining itself. It is a very weak, fragile institution.

And that is one of the reasons why doctrines like academic freedom have been concocted, given meaning, and spread in the most persuasive ways that could be devised—because that's about the university's only protection.

DR. MATHEWS: Perhaps the issue is really the character of the bond.

Dr. Wood: The point is that a university cannot simply accept a role as an agency or a business firm. It's a different kind of institution. How we negotiate and how we maintain our independence is really at the heart of the argument.

Dr. Goldwin: To get away from the Land of Oz, instead of talking of education simply, we can talk about all of the tax-exempt charitable organizations defined by law as distinct from other kinds of nongovernment corporations. They have been given a special standing in society. It is a public policy decision that many enterprises of great importance to the whole society will be run by nongovernment people. The need for that independence in universities and colleges is as great for the so-called public ones as for the so-called private ones.

Mr. Daly: Does this panel feel that academic freedom is not seriously threatened and has not been seriously invaded by government, except for the attempt to order the medical schools to admit a certain percentage of third-year people who had medical education overseas?

Dr. Graubard: We all agree on that instance, certainly. And one is very happy that a group of powerful institutions were willing to say no to that. And having said no, they found that the government acceded to that no. That is a clear instance.

Dr. Mathews: I think what we differ on is how to frame the case so as to have the public understand the grounds on which we differ. Some of us would frame the case in such a way as to talk about the university's distinctiveness. And distinctions do exist.

Others of us, who have the same concerns, would prefer to talk about similarities.

And the vigor with which we go at defining terms like "state" and "church" should not be misunderstood. Like all good members of the academy, we often go at issues in such a way as to give the impression that we are on utterly opposite sides when we are not.

DR. GOLDWIN: That's why the rest of the community never understands academic disputes.

FRED DELAQUADRY, dean of the School of Social Work, University of Alabama: I would like to ask a question on affirmative action. Statistics cited by the panelists give the impression that there hasn't been much gain in the objectives of bringing women and minorities into the universities. From my own experience this is not true. Statistics were cited up to 1972, but what about 1972 to 1978? Let me cite my school, a small part of the university. In 1972 we had about 32 percent women on the faculty. This past year, it was 55 percent as a result of affirmative action.

We had no blacks on our faculty in 1970 and 1972; today we have four full-time and two part-time. We were put into a position where we had to search out minority groups and bring them to the faculty. And we have succeeded in doing this.

Because of the federal government policy, which I think is correct on this at least, the situation has improved. Yet, from the statistics I have heard, the panelists don't seem to feel that there has been much improvement. Is this still true in 1978?

DR. WOOD: The data sources I was citing were the Lipset and Ladd faculty survey of August 1977 and the Carnegie Council Affirmative Action Report of 1976. I think the overall profiles show that, although women and blacks increased in absolute numbers, in terms of percentages and in the context of the total growth of the establishment, things remained about the same. Dr. Goldwin may have more information.

DR. GOLDWIN: The big change is occurring in undergraduate and graduate student proportions, and that will inevitably have its effect. But the controversy is not whether there is a change taking place; everybody can see the change. The question is whether the legislation is doing it and whether the legislation is doing other things that were unintended.

The whole process of faculty appointments, promotions, and tenure appointments has now become inextricably tangled with government regulation.

DR. MATHEWS: Let me just make a point to expand on what has been said. The question is, What method does the government use to advance this particular social end?

The sad conclusion one has to reach is that for a long time the policy of government was essentially to invest in legalistic maneuvers that moved the same number of women and minorities around from institution to institution, without increasing the number in the pool.

It was obvious that the composition of American higher education would not change, although it might change in one institution or another. Only recently has the federal government really begun to put its emphasis on increasing the numbers of women and minorities in graduate and professional schools. Until we are willing to do that seriously, we are engaging in an exercise in futility.

The proper argument is among people of the same conviction about the most effective way of achieving good ends.

DR. WOOD: David, we are now speaking a few weeks or months before the Bakke case comes to a conclusion. And depending on how that case goes, ways and means may be radically altered.

MR. DELAQUADRY: On rules and regulations, I happen to be in the School of Social Work, and the history of such schools shows that over 50 percent of their funding comes from the federal government. With that come rules and regulation. That doesn't have to be bad.

It becomes bad, as Dr. Mathews says, because of the way it is implemented. When Congress passes a law and delineates certain methods of imposing the law, some federal agency then proceeds to hire a staff to give out rules that go along with the law. The point is: How far should they go? In the case of our school, the federal government sets the standards and then the state agency that works with us takes those standards and imposes another set of rules and regulations.

I think we do have to be accountable, but the point is they are going too far in too many directions. They get involved in curriculum planning, in the kinds of appointments, in the areas of study.

I remember when Columbia Teachers College turned down a $10 million contract in education because it would not submit to the rules and regulations submitted by HEW.

MR. DALY: Let me interrupt for just a moment to ask one question. Has there not already developed in the body politic of education a degree of skill at defending academic freedom while at the same time meeting the complex responsibilities of government funding?

In the case of the third-year admissions in medical schools, and in the case of some relief from the safety and handicap regulations under affirmative action, the educational community has to use that dreadful expression "lobbied effectively on Capitol Hill."

Is not a solution to many of the problems which we have been discussing here a further development of these skills in the educational community, so that they get to legislation in its formative stage, before it becomes necessary to correct the harm already on the legislative books?

Dr. Mathews: I would say not.

Having participated in the various debates that you described, Mr. Daly—the debates over the foreign medical graduates and the handicapped regulations—I would have to report to the academic community that its force in the halls of politics is negligible, if not nonexistent.

And if the members of the educational community are under the illusion that they can rear up in their majesty and frighten off the Congress, they are mistaken. Nor should they think that Congress is necessarily ready to appropriate funds for the handicapped—as it logically should to follow the law's commitment to aid the handicapped. The fact is that the educational community has a good deal of political work yet to do.

Mr. Daly: Thank you.

This concludes another Public Policy Forum presented by the American Enterprise Institute for Public Policy Research. On behalf of AEI, our heartfelt thanks to the distinguished panelists, Dr. Robert Goldwin, Dr. David Mathews, Dr. Robert Wood, and Dr. Stephen Graubard, and, also, our thanks to our guests and experts in the audience for their participation. [Applause.]